Notes on the MIrror

Annalise Udell

BookLeaf Publishing

India | USA | UK

Presentation by *BookLeaf Publishing*

Web: www.bookleafpub.com

E-mail: info@bookleafpub.com

ISBN:9789358315691

First edition 2024

Apologies

I would like to issue a formal apology

I'm sorry that I didn't listen to you
Try to find a compromise
You see, I was dying
Not physically
Mentally
(I'm sorry for being dramatic)

I was sinking in something
Stress, maybe, or burnout
And you were too much to handle
Too much on my plate
(I'm sorry for making you feel guilty)

I couldn't possibly comprehend your pain
My head was muddled
I was so, so tired
(I'm sorry for making excuses)

And I couldn't see why your issue mattered so
much
When mine was never addressed
(I'm sorry for belittling your struggles)

When all I was to you was a punching bag

(I'm sorry for making you feel like you couldn't
talk to me)

But this apology isn't entirely for you
I am sorry to say that you are not the center of
the world
And I deserve kindness
Just as much
I don't need your permission
I can be kind to myself
And so, I would like to apologize
To a punching bag
To someone who was tired
To someone who was burnt out
To someone who was dying
I would like to apologize to myself on your
behalf
Because I know you never will

Precious Child

Innocence is bliss
Yet we give children Cupid's bow
And let them shoot
We tell them what they are to be
Who they are to love and how
What is expected of them
And tell ourselves that they have it easy
If I crumble
I, with only the weight of life on me
How can we expect children to be Atlas?
We hand them the expectations we've given them
The opinion of the world
Then scorn when they crumple
Perhaps a good gift for a baby shower
Would be something
Anything
To prop this horrid weight

My Broadway

My pencil tapping on the desk
Mimics the dancer's feet
The tympany player in my heart
Drums out a steady beat

The shouting of the passerby
Is the singers wailing away
Because life's a stage,
God bought a ticket
And this is my Broadway

The orchestra in the pit
Is the cars speeding down the road
I stomp my feet along the street
And sing as I walk home

I'll smile and curtsey for the people
But then I'll wave to you
I'll shout "come on, take a bow!
Because you were in this too!"

And then we'll bow together
And each go our own way
But I'm quite sure we'll meet again
Because this is our Broadway

Unreal

I stare at my hand
My hand?
A hand
Mine?
My… hand.
It feels disconnected
Like something could pass through it
Through living (ha) skin and flesh and bone
Like a ghost
Am I a ghost?
I don't feel alive
I don't feel real
I have responsibilities that cannot hold me
I've depended on that for so long and
now the rope has broken and
I'm floating away oh god I'm
floating away floating away floatingaway
My false hand has let go of what was tying me
to the ground
My shoes are in the air
My shoes?
Shoes.
Mine?
My… shoes.

Rain

Rain brings life
We are taught as children that water is life
So why are we taught that rain is sad?
Light is lovely
But too much can burn
The only times the rain has made my skin peel
Made me feel so ill that I couldn't move
Is when we poisoned it

The Shepherd

Abandoned by the gods
So I'll take the one they left me
I'll take her far away
I'll be her only devotee
Sing praises to her name
I'll call her hallelujah
Take my praises, my lord
Let them run right through you
You don't want a priest like me
Hands covered in your sacrifice
I'm sinking like a stone
Even though my heart is made of ice
Pull me onto the shore
You're the reason I breathe
As soon as I'm on the ground
I'm praying on my knees
Give me your stigmata
Make me the work of your hands
I'll tell the world I'm your worshiper
I'll follow your command
Like a lemming off the cliff
Like a lamb to the slaughter
Please just call me blessed
Make me your first martyr

Late Night

It's six am
I'm still awake
Nothing but noise on the TV
Fuels my dreams like a battery
Some rapper making it big
Don't know what he did
The channel flips
Blood drips
Another 2 dead
Fourteen more in hospital beds
Remote clatters down
Batteries rolling around
The unexpected
Can be so deadly
I fumble to put myself together
Keep this poison from turning my lungs to
leather
I try to care
Like reblog share
I'm not awake enough for this

A Sensual Reading

Lose yourself in my plot
Open your wings and soar
Fly away from reality
And into the blue

Dive into my pages
And enter a whole new world
Leave your problems behind
And stay for awhile

Run your fingers along my spine
And let the magic in
Let it consume you
And ignite something ancient inside

Delve into my world
And see yours in ruin
Know that only you can save it
But that you don't know how

Draw invisible masterpieces on my cover
And enter the coffee shop
See your soulmate
And feel your heart soar

Open the last one, you swear
And try to block the bullet
As he plunges to the ground
Taking your heart with him

Slam me shut
And ponder your choices
And the question that will keep you awake
into the night

Why do you torture yourself?
Why do you do this?
Why do you succumb to my story?
Why?
Why?

Bucket Filler

Big heart
I have a big heart
A full heart
A kind heart
It hurts when it beats
Oozing behind my ribs
You can see my skin flex
You can touch the bruises
It's too large for my chest
Too full of my blood
That's why I've got scars
To bleed out the love
I cut myself deep
When somebody asks
So many knives of favors
They fall out of my trash
My smile is bloody
My teeth are stained red
Done this too many times
I should be
I wish I was
I can't be
Dead

A knife

I have a knife
A sharp knife
A loving knife
In my chest
My shirt is stained
My sunday best
I gave and I gave
My heart was so full
I didn't know when to stop
My eyes are going dull
I tried so hard
Momma, I'm sorry
But now that I'm gone
You don't have to worry
I gave of myself
I gave too freely
Just one last time
You should
I wish you could
You can't
See me

Us

My generation is lazy
We're weak
We need our mommies to hold our hands
We're too sensitive
And we don't care
Because that makes sense
We're all freaks
Blue haired vegans
Spoken like that's a curse word
And we will never amount to what you were

That's because we're tired
We're so tired
Tired of wars you fund that we barely have a say
in
Tired of the news stories
"we're inheriting a world that you destroyed"
Tired of fighting
And fighting
And fighting
Everything is a fight
We fight to be heard
Fight to be acknowledged
Fight for our lives
Fight for our sanity

Every day is a battle

I'm sorry if I can't help lift the weight off of
your shoulders
My hands are sore from picking myself up by
my bootstraps
My fingers are slick with blood
My nails were ripped off when I clawed myself
out of the grave you dug
Our planet is so destroyed that we have no dirt
left to fill it in
Maybe we can use the rubble from the battles
you waged
Hear me
Hear me
Hear me

Or at least give me a shovel

Notes on the MIrror

Colorful papers
Small reassurances
You are enough
Please keep fighting
I love you
Color marring my reflection
Covering my image
I am enough?
Keep fighting?
You love me?

They help on occasion
Covering up the nasty things
One over my stomach
Another concealing my shoulder
A third hiding the dark bags

But some days
It seems that they define me
I am hollow
Light as a breeze
Empty affirmations easily swept away
Paper is not an anchor, dear

On the worst days, they cut

I'm not worthy of what they say
I can't believe their lies
Neon paper shining on my sins
The hurt to look at
Hurt to read
I hate that they help
Paper is not an anchor
But it can be a chain

A Song of Revolution

I'll sing you a song of anger
Each verse shall be an injustice.
A freedom that we have yet to experience
As we remember those who think you and I mad

I'll sing you a song of restlessness
Of whispers through the town
Messengers dancing across the dawn
As we remember a people -- prepared to greet
death

I'll sing you a song of battle
Of swords and words clashing day and night
People who were not soldiers running off to war
As we remember a fight for the freedom we
craved

I'll sing you a song of loss
Of bodies cradled by family, friends, and lovers
Of cries echoing through the night
As we remember fighting off the doubt creeping
in

I'll sing you a song of victory
Of tasting freedom for the first time

Praying that our song would not fall on deaf ears
As we raise a glass to a future that does not
repeat the past

Sunset Hearts

Cloaked in cloth the colors of the sunset
I reach my hand out
And grab a hand unnaturally white
Covered in tears.
Broken phrases fly through my head
Phrases of hate and rejection
Phrases of desperation and confusion
Phrases from a mouth that only wants
acceptance.

Reaching down the other hand
To pull up a girl
Who looks dangerously unreal
But painfully familiar.
I look in this mirror
tainting my past
Pull the girl into a tight embrace
Trying to convey
She is a survivor.
Girl with a sunset heart
You can take solace
In the version of yourself that stands before you.

Disappointment

Disappointment disappointment
I am nobody's daughter
The lamb saw the knife
Walked away from the slaughter

Disappointment disappointment
I am nobody's son
The moon cartwheeled across the sky
When the day was done

Disappointment disappointment
I am nobody's lover
I forgot to kiss her softly
As I moved above her

Disappointment disappointment
I am nobody's friend
I abandoned the station
That I was supposed to tend

Disappointment disappointment
I'm sick of my own lies
What does the mirror see
when it meets my eyes

Disappointment disappointment
Put an end to me now
I've finished holding out
Let me take my bow

I'm nobody's daughter
I'm nobody's son
I'm nobody's family
When the day is done

I'm nobody's lover
I'm nobody's friend
I've performed my waltz
Let this tragedy end

Disappointment disappointment
I am nobody's performer
If she can't stand the sight of blood
Be sure to warn her

Disappointment disappointment
I'm your entertainment
This poor disappointment
Is staining the pavement

The Villain's Journey

It will always be the same
Life is a cycle
Every time we meet
We battle across the skyline
I'm a maniac, haven't you heard?
A psychopath
Shunned by the very people who shattered me
And you're a hero
A paradigm
What I would look like whole, I think
And we'll fight again
And again
And again
And you'll win again
And again
And again
Because the sun will always rise to banish the
darkness
Cyclical

I think I could stop our cycle
If I really wanted to, that is
I could stop fighting you
Simply step away before I step onto the roof
But I'll always leap

Plunge into my next grand scheme
and wait for you to stop me
Because oh, darling, if you're the sun
Then I'm Icarus
I can't help but fly close to you
And if I fall again
And again
And again
Then at least I get to see you
The only person who has ever cared
Cared enough to greet me again
And again
And again
Cyclical

Executive Misfunction

I'm paralyzed
(It's not an excuse)
Glued to my phone
(It's not an excuse)
Can't stop the doomscroll
(It's not an excuse)
Can't shut off my alarm
(It's not an excuse)
Can't move
(It's not)
Can't breathe
(An)
Flatlining

Posters

I'm not allowed to have posters
I never was
Tape ruins the paint
I didn't want them anyways
I had a frame here and there
Some art that my friends made
Important certificates and medals
Things that wouldn't rip when you took them
down
I had life on every flat surface
Graded assignments
Old bottles that I liked
A jar full of my tips
Countless hair ties
Bits and bobs and whatchamacallits
My living has always been fluid
You can take things off a nail and put them back
up
You can clear away the bits and bobs
A poster has always seemed permanent
Peeling tape and ripping paper meant death

I never liked stickers
I never knew what to put them on
Or I did decide and I didn't know where

There were too many choices
I couldn't fit them anyways
My notebook covers had doodles
Notes for classes they weren't for
My water bottle was scuffed and scratched
The rubber handle full of graphite-lined holes
My binders had papers shoved in the front
I didn't take my computer anywhere
And I could barely ride my skateboard
A sticker has always seemed too permanent
Because the items they were stuck to would be
thrown away

Maybe this says something about me
I'm not sure

I started putting stickers on my water bottle

Work of Art

I wish I had someone
Who would use my skin as a canvas
Take this marker
Vent your frustrations across my back
Write a love poem on my legs
Send flowers swirling across my arms
I want to feel a gentle touch
The drag of a pen
The quiet love in the air
I want to see their gentle smile
Please dear God
Just let me make them smile

Instead I get this
This canvas of my pain
Take these fists
Beat bruises into my back
Walk away from here with my legs
Send scratches scrawling across my arms
All I feel is a sharp pain
The drag of my feet
The screaming anger in the air
All I see is my teary-eyed reflection
Please dear God
Just let me make them smile

Mask

When I was twelve
I made a mask
It wasn't very good
The old colors were visible
if you looked hard enough
The one that I chose was gray and purple,
though
I was safe
I thought I was safe
But I had to get a new mask
It was hastily painted
It scared me so
And I let the colors show
I made sure it was painted better after that

I've been so desperate
All this time
To paint the mask
No matter what color it is
White and black paint has stained my hands
My mind
My soul
I just want my colors
I'm so tired of paint
I've spent so much of myself buying it

And one day
I'll run out
I'll be empty
Me and a half-painted mask

Hurts

It hurts to watch you smile
Because I know how tight it is
How fake
A mask would look more real
But I'm the only one who can tell
I see your bleeding heart
I hear you sing my name like a love letter
Help me
Hurt me
Love me
Hate me
My dear you needn't ask
You only need to take off that false smile
Let me see the dried tear tracks
Let me stitch your heart
And clean the blood from your giving hands
You've done so well
Let me give you rest

Scream

I want to scream
So often do I want to scream
But volume is so frowned upon
Especially from a young woman
So I rip the scream from my throat
And use it as ink
Listen to me, damn you!
I take that volume from the air
And put it on a page
I would scream if I could
But I can't
So i write
Let those who stand by me murmur
I know you're scared my love
Whisper your rage into my ear and let me
scream for you
Those who stand against us will scream into the
air
Let them
Pages last longer